YOUR PERSONAL GUIDE TO TRUE SELF-LOVE

Lashonda E. Hollins, LCSW

ISBN: 978-1-7350277-0-8 (Paperback)
ISBN: 978-1-7350277-1-5 (eBook)

Any references to historical events, real people, or real places are used fictitiously. Names, characters, and places are products of the author's imagination.

Front cover image by Abdul Latif Ripon
Book design by Lashonda E. Hollins

First Printing Edition: May 2020

Publisher: L. Hollins S.P.E.A.K.S
San Antonio, Texas 78254

www.lhollinsspeaks.com

TABLE OF CONTENTS

3

DEDICATION

To my parents:

Firstly, to my mother who left so soon and so suddenly. I've only ever wished for two things in life; that you are proud of me and that I shall one day see you again. I love you dearly and miss you, Mary Ann.

To my father who never stopped believing in me and always pushed me to be the best I could be, this book is a proud piece that I dedicate to you for all your support and all you sacrificed to get me here. I love you, Daddy.

WHAT DOES IT FEEL LIKE?

What does it feel like to be you?

What does it feel like to wake up every morning knowing that you are authentic and true? you are just YOU.

What does it feel like knowing that you are enough? Knowing that even on the day you scream, yell, fight, and fuss, you and your life are still enough.

What does it feel like to choose yourself? Taking everything and everyone and placing their needs on a shelf

What does it feel like?

What does it feel like to read and see something in your life that could never be?

I have a husband, children, and a job to keep

Never in a million years could I just choose

me.

What does it feel like?

To be lost at sea?

Do you see me?

Can't I be free?

What would happen if I just chose me? Not

every day, just for today.

To take a moment and do things my way,

acknowledge my needs, wants, and desires.

To step outside the box and aim higher.

What would it feel like?

GETTING TO KNOW THE AUTHOR

"To know me is to love me and to accept my flaws and all."-L. Hollins

I always knew I was an over achiever and I worked really hard to be great at everything I did. I always noticed that stagnation was a problem, patience was non-existent, and feeling like I needed to do more was constant. It wasn't until I started reading a book by Rachel Hollis titled, "Girl Stop Apologizing" that I realized I had learned to be an overachiever from childhood. I realized at an early age that success gave me the attention I needed to feel great about myself. I received attention through achievements as a child. I knew if I got good grades or if I got an award, my parents would be there cheering me on. It wasn't until that moment that I realized my life was shaped even before I realized it.

Even as a 32 years old woman, I am still an overly active social butterfly and that sometimes gets the best of me because I overbook myself quite often. I wasn't always this social butterfly that believed I could do anything. I remember vividly in middle school, feeling like I just wanted to fit in, be popular, and be pretty. The truth is I never really struggled to make friends but in my head what I had wasn't enough. I constantly compared myself to others, what they looked like, and what they had. Now I know none of that really mattered because I was already beautiful inside and out. Being, what I thought at the time, a chubby tomboyish little girl, I didn't possess the highest self-esteem. One summer I consciously decided I was going to lose weight. I secretly did workouts in my room and I didn't over eat or indulge; if you are from the south, you'd know this is hard. Whenever I felt hungry, I would force myself to take a nap instead of giving in to the hunger and cravings that rushed through my body. Looking back at the steps I took, for a 15-year-old at that time, seemed healthy, as I know it could have been worse. Mentally it was still just as damaging. The unfortunate part is that even at that age, I'd somehow fixated on my weight and associated being skinny with pretty and lighter skin. I know there are young girls who resort to much more harmful ways of trying to fit in or lose weight, so I am not saying my way was the absolute worst, but the fact is the mentality is the same and that is unhealthy. During this time, I remember not wanting anyone to know I was working out which was why I only worked out in my room. Thinking about it now, I feel sad for my 15-year-old self. I wasn't losing weight to be healthy; I was losing weight to be pretty.

Fast forward to the start of the new school year. I was finally in 9th grade and finally in high school. I'd lost so much weight it was the first thing people noticed. I remember one male student asking me (at age 15) if I had AIDS? Side note: kids can be cruel. Please talk to your kids and make sure they are uplifting each other and not tearing each other down. These kids are growing up to be adults and they truly are the next generation. Now, back to my first day of school. I had finally lost the weight and I felt like I could now fit in, boy was I wrong. You know how people say, "if it ain't one thing it's another?" That statement is so true. There is and will always be something. I was now a size 5 teenager with DD breast trying to squeeze into a C cup bra, a flat butt, and exotropia (when one or both eyes turn outward) ... which all the kids called cock-eyed. Also, I am sure you are thinking what does a "flat butt" have to do with anything? but being black and having no curves is almost a taboo and people are not afraid to point it out. When you are a child that hurts just like any other negative thing a person says to you or about you.

It was in high school that I became more of an over achiever. I was able to get amazing grades, be Student of the Week, be a member of Student Council, Newspaper Staff, SADD Club, Year Book Staff, Basketball

Book Keeper, as well as play Soccer. All of these things made me feel amazing...accomplished so to speak. These things came with compliments from adults and my peers and It was exhilarating. Being this active fueled something inside of me. I graduated Senior Class President and Historian of my class, which is third in the class. I was inducted into the School Hall of Fame upon my graduation. So many people were proud of me in my senior year. Not only were my parents proud but the entire black community was proud as well. Being black, being a top 3 graduate, and being ready for college was a big deal in the small town of Mendenhall, Mississippi. This experience continued to fuel my need to achieve.

I wanted to start with this particular story of my life, not to boast or brag, but because it wasn't until years later that I learned the true meaning of loving myself. I went through life seeking validation for my achievements from other people. I accomplished great things in college as well but I went through both grad school and undergrad still trying to find my place and find love for myself. This doesn't mean that I am no longer an over achiever it just means I do what makes me happy and I don't need the validation of anyone else to be in my happy place. Shifting from societal validation to self-validation is not an easy feat but worth every tough experience. Being able to find self-love and self-validation is a beautiful thing and that is what I plan to share with you in this book. I plan to share with you steps I have taken and moments I have experienced that have been the most impactful on my life. What I would hope is you can start your path to complete self-love through reading this guide.

Once you have obtained true self-love no one can control you, anyone can hate you, and most importantly no one can make you feel guilty for being exactly who you are. Thank you for trusting me to share my story with you. Toni Morrison, a great novelist, stated when "you are free, you need to free

16

somebody else. If you have some power, then your job is to empower somebody else." That is what I want to do with this book. I want to empower all of the women like me, those coming up behind me, and those who encounter someone like me.

I am no expert. I am only experienced, and from my experiences comes both mine and your knowledge and strength.

CHAPTER ONE

What is Self-Love?

"Believing that you are just as important as they are, that's self-love." L. Hollins

According to Webster, the definition of self-love pertains to promoting your own welfare or well-being with an excessive regard for one's own advantage. It also describes self-love as conceit and vanity. It even goes as far as using the word "narcissism" to describe this beautiful term we call self-love. I am not a fan of these definitions by any means especially the last two definitions. The idea of loving myself being narcissistic or vain is complete and utter bull crap. I prefer to create my own definition for the purpose of this book. So here is how I see and how we shall see the term for the remainder of this book. Self-love is one's ability to recognize and accept they are perfectly made, flaws and all, and love themselves regardless. Self-love is knowing when you can't fill anyone else's cup because it is time to fill your own. Self-love is knowing when it is okay to choose yourself for your own well-being and believing that you, your wants, and your needs are just as important as theirs. It is not about personal gain or advantage it is about loving yourself enough to be completely comfortable with choosing yourself when necessary.

It is hard to mention self-love and not mention self-care. So many of us get wrapped up in being the perfect wife, the perfect mother, daughter, sister, or friend. We rarely stop to think about our own wellbeing, let alone our own hopes, dreams, and aspirations. Don't get me wrong there's nothing wrong with these roles but each one of those roles are service roles. You are being something to and for someone else. At what point do you say, "today is my day?" It is so easy to get lost in these roles and forget who you are in the process. Once you have lost yourself, it leaves the door open for resentment. You start to resent the very same people you are trying to take care of.

20

You resent your husband for having more free time than you or that he was able to complete the degree you've been dying to complete. Resentment can eat away at you and your relationships one day at a time.

When discussing resentment in relationships there is a hard pill to swallow and I hope you are ready for it. Here is the shocker; truth 101. You are a part of the problem. Yes, I said it. You, my friend, are part of the problem. Ask yourself how many times have I said, "No you go ahead. I can handle it" or "It's okay you go out. I'll stay in" or "No, I don't need anything and yes I can handle it." How many times? All of this is happening when on the inside you are

21

screaming; I need a break. Mentally you are feeling like you may crack at any given moment but you continue to say you have it all under control. You may have it under control but where are you emotionally, mentally, and physically? I used to hear my mom and aunts say all the time "I'm about to have a nervous breakdown." I never actually knew what that looked like or what it entailed but as I grew, I got to realize a nervous breakdown looks like a panic attack. This comes from an absurd amount of stress, feeling overwhelmed, and feeling like you are losing control. Many of us are on our way to a nervous breakdown because we are not properly caring for ourselves. It is sad to think some people view self-care and self-love as what Webster calls narcissistic and vain. That is not the case at all. Self-love and self-care are necessary. As I typed this book, an old friend came to mind. I remembered a moment when her own world was crashing around her. Work, life, health and relationships all around her were failing and as I tried to motivate and encourage her into loving herself and seeing herself as worthy, somehow, she still wanted to talk about the people in her life that she was pouring so much of herself into. I stressed to her that there is no way she can fill any of their cups from an empty cup which was her own. It was illogical and it was hard for me to watch

23

as a friend.

In all honesty and complete transparency, I too have fallen victim to this way of thinking. When my mom died, I did everything I could possibly do to keep her memory alive. My mom was like the glue of our family, she held together so many small pieces with not just our immediate family but our extended family as well. I can't imagine how stressful that must have been for her but I can tell you how stressful it was for me. Once she died, I tried to pick up the torch and fill those shoes. All along those shoes were too big and never mine to fill to begin with. I never properly grieved my mother's death (which later caught up with me) because I was too busy trying to keep the world spinning. I rolled right into trying to be everything to everyone. When there was an argument in the family I was called, if something needed to be done, I was called, if I was needed to travel, I traveled. I planned gatherings and get-togethers, pictures, and birthdays and yes, I even planned my wedding in the midst of what would have been the end of the world for a normal 23-year-old. I was trying to be and do everything my mom had done, finish undergrad, complete grad school, and get a good job. It wasn't until 3 years later that my breakdown came. I was driving, alone, in my new car, coming from my new job 2 states away from

25

my family, and I just started to sob (Thanks to Miranda Lambert's song Over You). I was sobbing for absolutely no reason and I didn't know what was wrong with me. I had to pull over to gather myself. When I got home, I looked at my husband and told him, "I think I am depressed and have been for a while." Being a new therapist at the time myself, this was major. It was at that time I realized I was stretching myself thin and I needed to find a way to change the projection of my life. I was trying to give when I had nothing to give. I was completely out of energy and when I think back to that time in my life I was overeating and unhealthy. I knew I had to stop being available for everyone else's needs and/or drama, I had to accept that my mother was gone and I could not fill her shoes. I had to accept that nothing would ever be the same. I still struggle today with knowing nothing will ever be exactly the way it was. When I notice I am absorbing way more than I should from surrounding situations I process and determine whether or not it is okay to step away. What I say when it comes to my mental, physical and emotional health is it's okay to be selfish to save my life. Are you ready to save your life?

CHAPTER TWO
You Have to Do the Work

"The work you do means something. Be proud of that work."-L. Hollins

The work you put in means something. The work you put in makes a difference and deserves to be acknowledged. The problem lies in just getting started.

So, what have I done to start the process of building the skills I need to reach complete self-acceptance and love? First, I had to acknowledge that I wanted to work on being a better me. I had to admit there were areas I could grow in. I started with reading motivational books just like I am writing for you today. I listened to brave and strong people whom I admired not just for what they have accomplished but also for whom they are as people. I watched Maya Angelou and gazed at the television in awe as I absorbed so much of her wisdom and knowledge. I watched Michelle Obama, the first black First Lady of the United States, stand firm and true to who she is even as many called her monkey, manly, and other awful names or slurs. I watched, as she never came down from her happy place to meet people who disliked her at their miserable place. She loved herself so much she didn't let any of the hatred sway her. Her unyielding poise in any situation is the epitome of self-love. This was a true inspiration. Watching, learning, and listening are important throughout this process. It's easier to speak than it is to listen. I continue to do this work even today. Watching inspirational videos, listening to inspirational presentations, and reading books, all of this helps me continue to stand firm in who I am.

Starting out as a young black female in the professional world, I allowed people to tell me I was too assertive, too blunt, or too active. I must admit it would bother me, remember, I preferred attention from achievement. I would always try to make the necessary changes in myself that would make others more comfortable with my go-getter yet over achieving personality. My intentions are never to hurt anyone in my boldness, bluntness, or assertiveness but I have also learned intimidation is not my problem. That is their problem. What I mean by that is, people can and will be intimidated by strong personalities and won't know how to deal with it, and let's be honest, even more so when you are black. The safest and easiest way for them to understand and deal with it is to see it as negative or bad and blame you for their uncomfortableness. I have experienced it and I have seen it happen to others. I have witnessed person after person resign because someone else was intimidated by their personality. My response to that now is NOT TODAY! You will not make me feel bad for just being me. You will not make me feel bad for having a voice or an opinion. You will not make me feel bad for standing out. When you know, accept, and love who you are no one else can cast their doubts and fears on you. Another person's problem is not our learning curve and we can no longer assume responsibility for that. We have to learn to not allow people to place their insecurities on us.

The key to being successful in this stage of your growth and doing the work is being 100% honest with yourself. This is an absolute necessity. It is important to have the ability to admit when you are wrong and call yourself on your own bull crap. Don't stand firm in a situation in which you know in your heart was wrong or you know the action was meant for ill will. Don't allow self-mediocrity in anything you do. Don't be afraid to apologize, admit fault when there is fault, and know you didn't lose but you grew. Don't be afraid to be you.

It is also imperative to know not everyone will understand your process and not everyone will make it through your journey but it is one you must take whether they come along or not. There will be people you encounter who don't want to see you grow or will try to shame you for your growth and learning to love yourself. Sometimes that means they are losing something in your learning to love yourself they know they'll never get back. This might be you learning to say no to them or just your inability to be where they need you to be when they want you to be there. If the people in your life truly love you and care about your wellbeing they will understand and support you throughout the process.

There is one more type of person to be on the lookout for during your growth process. Let's be clear when you are working to become a better person and something inside you starts to shift, people notice. Be aware of those people in this world who will continue to bring up your past and try to tear you down and hurt you with it. These persons treat you as if you could never change and will do everything in their power to not only convince you but anyone else who will listen. They will do all they can to keep you exactly where you are. Don't let these people prevent you from doing the work you need to do in your life. Once you have reached a place of self-love these persons will no longer be able to use your past to hurt you. Why? Because at this point you will not only love yourself but you will ACCEPT yourself, flaws and all. Once you are there, people can no longer use those flaws against you. What they have to say about you won't matter. With that being said I am here to tell you to be intentional with your plans, do the work, make the changes, and trust yourself. Your past doesn't define you rather your future, the constant work you put in does.

Chapter Recap

This chapter had some very important points and I want to make sure you are aware of what those are and keep them near and dear as you go through this process. Below I have highlighted some of the main take away points.

1. Acknowledge.

2. Admit.

3. Watch, Learn, Listen.

4. Their feeling intimidated by your true and authentic personality

isn't your problem.

5. Be 100% honest with yourself.

6. Admit when you are wrong, apologize, and grow.

7. No self-mediocrity.

8. Your past doesn't define you, your constant work does.

CHAPTER THREE
Adopting the Right Disposition

- Through Your Eyes

As I started to write this book, I thought it would be interesting to look at how some of my friends viewed self-love and how or even if they implement their own self-love. This turned into a very small qualitative study for me because I assumed many were not implementing true self-care but I did assume they'd think self-love was positive and much needed. I first asked a very simple question, "What would you think if you heard someone say, 'I love myself'?" I was pretty amazed that of the 21 women who were brave enough to respond, all of the answers were extremely positive and very similar. I'd like to note that this post was available to men as well as women but not one male responded. Responses consisted of all women saying things like, "I'd say that person is confident, that person has accepted and embraced themselves completely, that's awesome we don't hear that enough, that person understands life, that person went through something and their self-love was tested, and I wish more people felt this way about themselves." Only 3 of the 21 women said something slightly different. One person stated she wouldn't think anything because some people only say those words for a response, stating she would instead respond to the writer and ask how they came to love themselves and that is what would catch her attention. That particular answer was shocking for me because here we had someone saying to hear another person say they loved themselves could mean they were almost attention seeking. I can't say for certain this is what she meant but if I read that anywhere else that's how I would feel. This is one of the stigmas attached to self-love that I'd like to change. Learning to love yourself is not seeking attention from others instead it is learning to give yourself the same time and attention you give others.

Another respondent stated it depends

on what she is looking at when the person makes the statement, but the standout response was from the final respondent who said she'd think the person doesn't feel loved by others so they are saying it to themselves. This one was a powerful statement because often times people who are working on self-love have struggled to do so in the past. They have struggled to not only love themselves but even feel deserving of the love of others around them. They may have unconsciously ignored themselves for so long and consistently held the wants and needs of others above their own while rarely receiving that attention back from those same individuals. So, this respondent was on to something. Saying positive things to yourself and verbalizing your love for yourself even when you don't feel deserving or when you fear others will judge you is the hard part but it is also where the work begins.

In doing this little question and answer I followed the above question with a second question. I asked, "in the last 2 months how many of you have literally taken the time to love yourself? Legitimately love yourself without the inclusion of anyone else or your happiness being dependent on someone else? Taken time away from being a wife, a mommy, a sister, a friend, etc. and just focus on yourself and what you want?" I only had

15 people respond this time. I knew I would have some attrition because this question is a little more personal and asks people to take a look at themselves and their own life. It is asking them to take a look at how they treat themselves and if thinking deep enough it could also pose the question of how am I being treated by those around me. Out of the 15 people 8 of them, which is more than half, stated they have not taken any time for themselves in the last year. It was very interesting because one respondent stated that it was on the 1st of the year (2019) that she started to truly love herself and take time for herself. She stated, "I vowed to not let other people control my

life...I was used to being there for everyone and after my mom passed, honestly I was too drained to be what someone else needed me to be. I put me 1st and for those that walked away because I said I can't, I've learned to be okay with that instead of beating myself up over it." What this respondent experienced is what I am trying to get women to see in this book. I want you to see the importance of implementing self-love and self-care in your daily life before things start to fall apart or you are at your wits end.

I know the above is a small sample size but it still shows a clear correlation between women and how very few create time for themselves in their daily life.

- Get Out of Your Way

One of my biggest pet peeves and something that I have tried to remove from my vocabulary is the phrase "that's the way I have always done it." This one phrase is the bane of not just my existence but all of our existence. This simple statement can cause so much self-sabotage and complacency, it's unreal. This statement, simply put, holds us back and prevents us from moving forward. To be honest with you, we utter these words for quite a few reasons. One of those reasons would be fear...fear of what's to come, fear of taking a big leap and failing, or fear of facing true change. We doubt

45

ourselves quite often and that is a fact. So, what if you fail? What would life really be like if you started to put yourself first? What would people really think? WHO CARES! It doesn't matter what they think; it only matters how you feel when you look at yourself in the mirror. So here is the secret, home girl, if you can walk past that mirror and love yourself through and through knowing you gave 100% to being the best possible person you can be, then SO WHAT!

We also use these words when we are lazy and don't want to put any additional effort into a task or when it's easy to just use what we already have. Another reason is when there is a lack of knowledge, when we don't know what this change can really do for us. I want to provide an example. I worked with someone who used this phrase as a rebuttal anytime anyone tried to bring up a new idea or process improvement. It was obvious that the reason for saying it was a combination of fear, doubt, and lack of knowledge. Fear that they would look bad if they didn't have the knowledge, fear of having to ask someone for help or looking bad to our superiors, and the constant doubt that it could even be pulled off before putting in any effort. It was always one of the most frustrating encounters of my week. The truth was things may have looked as if they were working, but we were stagnating and

47

things weren't getting better. The way it had always been may have worked in the 80s but it was definitely not what we needed for the twenty-first century. I know what you are thinking, if it works then why change it? But my question to you is, IS IT REALLY WORKING? This is the self-sabotage and negative mentality we can get caught in quite often; thinking that something is working until we learn the hard way it isn't. So again, is it really working? Have you made the changes you want to make or done the things you want to do?

When we are talking about getting out of our own way it doesn't mean that you don't have a great family or great memories or have succeeded in providing your family with the best life experiences possible. We are talking specifically about you and your needs, wants, and dreams. This is where you have to get real with yourself and identify if you are truly being intentional in the decisions that you are making for yourself. Remember, when you are truly at your best, your entire family benefits from that. If you know what you have been doing isn't working and you are just going through the motions to make the lives of other people better, then why stay where you are? Why not make a change that benefits you and them?

The way to impact, growth, happiness,

and self-love is stepping outside of that comfort zone and doing something different, trying new things, taking new risks, and trusting that the new journey you are on is worth it. Be intentional with those new things and know what it is you want for yourself. We have to get over getting use to stuff! Getting use to stuff or complacent in situations is one of the main things that prevent us from moving forward and getting out of our own way. The key to getting out of our own way is not being complacent, not being afraid, lazy, or taking the easy way out, but instead being intentional, combating our biases, and improving our own wellbeing.

- Gratitude

Now, let's talk a little more about the importance of showing gratitude. Gratitude is when you can look around and be grateful and thankful for all the things you have in your life. Especially those small things that we often times overlook and tend to take for granted. It is so easy to get caught up in all that is going wrong in our lives that we convince ourselves into believing nothing good is happening in our lives. I can assure you and would bet my bottom dollar that something good is happening in your life and in my life every single day. If you were having a bad day and a stranger smiled and greeted you, people, that is something to be thankful for. The stranger that held the door for you today when your hands were full...thank God for that man! Small acts of kindness are happening every single day in our lives and it is up to us to notice them. When you can notice those moments, it is those small things that can change the entire projection of your day and eventually your life. Statistically, gratitude can change the way you view the world and all of your relationships

Why is this something I am sharing in a book about self-love? I'll tell you why. Being grateful for the small things allows us to focus on being the best versions of ourselves. When we focus on the negative things going on around us it triggers negative think, negative self-talk, and can cause a decline in the way we see ourselves. It can so easily take you from feeling like today is a horrible day to I can never do anything right and I am a horrible person. When we take time to focus on all the little things, we won't have time to dwell on the negative. THIS is what gratitude and small acts of kindness can change. How? Because we are spending our time focusing on the things that matter. We are focusing on nothing but the facts, everything else is assumption. Don't get lost in a world of negativity and assumption. When you have the facts right in your face, you just have to notice them.

CHAPTER FOUR
Be Open to Feedback

"Feedback is for the champions of the world."-L. Hollins

Feedback is HARD but a necessary part of growth. If you are not receiving feedback you are not truly growing. Now, the type of feedback you are receiving and who you are receiving it from is key. Therefore, I have to start this chapter with telling you what I believe to be the two types of feedback and why one is meant to provide confidence, growth and elevation while the other is meant to tear you down, destroy your confidence, and shatter your dreams. True feedback from a true leader is monumental.

It's no secret I strive to be the best leader I can possibly be. Through self-education, observation, and leadership opportunities I am slowly building the skills I need to grow as a future leader. One of the opportunities I had a couple years ago was to attend a 2-week leadership training. With this training we had to do self-assessments as well as send assessments of our supervisor and a few of our coworkers. Eager to get started and see what people thought of me as a co-worker and employee, I sent the email explaining anonymity and what was expected of them in completing the assessment. I even walked round the office providing reminders. Once the deadline had passed and the assessments were complete, I received my anonymous results. For the most part my coworkers thought I was great as well as my supervisor. The consensus was; I was a hard worker, great leader, and always willing to help. BUT there was a free hand section where someone (whom I swear to this day I know who it was due to history) wrote "She likes to be the center of attention and is mean to her coworkers. She is great with the clients though." Talk about knocking the wind out of my sail. Of all the amazing things that were said about me this stood out to me because it was not worded in a way that was meant to be positive or change provoking. This was worded in a manner that was meant to be hurtful. I realized that right away. I immediately wanted to approach the person I KNEW had written it. Luckily, I had some great people to lean on who encouraged me to take a step back, accept that I had no real proof it was that person, and identify what I could take from this particular situation. I had another co-worker and in her free hand section someone wrote, she has been in America for a long time. She needs to learn to speak English better. My immediate thought was people are so brave behind keyboards and anonymity. They say things they would never say to your face that are meant to tear you down completely. Positive feedback is meant to be presented in a way that is change promoting and thoughtful. These people had other hidden agendas and it stuck out like a sore thumb. Myself and my coworker supported each other through this confusing time but the truth is other people's opinions can sometimes undermine our view of self.

Weeks later the actual leadership training began and we had to process these results aloud. The easy thing to do would have been to not mention this particular feedback at all. Instead I used it as an inspiration. I processed this information with my leadership class and instructor and we all felt the feedback was not positive. I was able to admit that I am an overachiever and active in several things in the work place but that is not equivalent to wanting to be the center of attention. That specifically came from a place of jealousy. After this 2-weeks class, I came out inspired by my own story. I knew I didn't want any other goal chasers and trendsetters to feel what I felt. I never wanted them to question themselves and feel they have to dim their light in order for someone else's to shine. It was my mission to make sure that didn't happen.

The following year I was asked to come back and present in one of those same leadership classes. I chose to educate that group of future leaders on knowing the difference between positive and negative feedback. My topic was Self-Assessment and Handling Constructive Criticism. Criticism is part of life and there is no way around it. People will give you feedback whether you request it or not. Normal criticism is simply an expression of disapproval that can be hurtful and lower self-confidence and self-esteem. An example would be older people who love saying, "You getting fat aintcha?" As if we would really say yes, ma'am I sure am. It's funny thinking about it now but it is an example of unsolicited feedback or criticism. This is the type of feedback we have to learn and know when to ignore. Constructive criticism is made with the goal of generating change in you for the better it's meant to be improving. Negative feedback and criticism are meant to be harmful even if the person isn't aware that they are hurting you.

The goal here is to surround yourself with people who want to see you grow and prosper. Surround yourself with friends and family who will be completely open and honest with you but in a positive way; a way that will bolster you into the person you are meant to be. I try to be this type of friend. Because of my assertiveness and my bluntness, I am very honest with my friends. I try to find balance because I don't want to sound like a "know it all" friend or someone who thinks they have all of the answers because I don't. I have also had to find balance between listening and speaking. Receiving any kind of feedback isn't easy but if your delivery is meant to take your friend or family member to the next level then you are on the right track.

If you are truly open to feedback and can take it and make something amazing with it, then you are ready to move forward. Constructive feedback is truly the breakfast of champions. Eat it up and let it give you all you need to grow strong and be successful.

How to Open Yourself Up to Positive Feedback

Yikes! Being vulnerable and opening

yourself up to any kind of criticism is scary. You picture a round table of people telling you everything you suck at. This is definitely an unrealistic view. If you have taken the above steps to surround yourself with strong positive people, then you know you can trust what they say. I have a handful of friends I can call and say, "Tell me, was I wrong?" I know they will shoot me straight with no chaser but from a place of love. So often, we choose to go to people for advice who will tell us what we want to hear as opposed to the real truth and that is setting yourself up for failure. A true and honest friend will tell you the truth even if it may hurt in a way that doesn't break you or make you feel awful.

The key here is knowing as well as accepting that you are not perfect and trusting the process of change. A natural reaction to someone giving you feedback is anger, frustration, or shame. The natural reaction to change is fear. It all feels like you have failed at something even when you didn't. Trust the process and trust the people you handpicked. Trust they are only adding to something you are already excelling at, and yes, you are excelling even if you are just starting because you took the first step. You have not failed; you have only just begun. With self-assessment, good positive feedback, and doing the work, you are already breaking down barriers towards complete self-love.

CHAPTER FIVE
"That's Not for Me."

"Anything you set out to do IS for you."-L. Hollins

Several times in my life I have made the statement "That's not for me" and several times in my life I have been wrong. I use to say natural hair isn't for me and 3 years ago I did "the big chop." I use to say locs weren't for me and 4 months ago I started the starter loc process. I use to say I am not a runner or a jogger and this year alone I have run three 5K runs and currently looking for more. So many times, I have doubted my beauty and my capabilities and so many times I have been wrong. In every single one of those things I feared failure. I feared failure so much that several times it prevented me from starting. Once I realized I wasn't going to worry about validation from anyone other than myself my courage increased tremendously. Once I developed the courage to take that leap, I defied all of the odds. Many times, we doubt ourselves. We say things aren't for us out of fear and walking away from it is much easier than taking the leap. Part of self-love comes from trusting yourself and trusting that failure is a part of life. Trusting that failure at a task doesn't mean you, the person, is a failure. Failure is a necessity. Why is failure a necessity? Because it teaches you way more than you could ever imagine. You have insight on what you did wrong and what needs improvement. It shows you that though you didn't get that job you took the step, interviewed, and the sky didn't fall in the process.

Failure is an overachiever's worst nightmare and honestly, it took me until 2 years ago to accept the idea that failure is part of my growth. I ran from things that scared me and if I didn't get the job, I was angry. I questioned myself and the interviewer's intelligence as well. Through my trying to find something better I failed along the way and now I know failure is okay. I'd honestly gone through my entire life setting goals and reaching them...consistently. So, when I got to a point in my life, adult life, and I wasn't always winning, I wasn't getting jobs on the first interview, struggling with women's health issues, or just felt situations weren't going my way or living up to my expectations I was shocked. I'd already fallen into a depression due to being overweight and not happy with person I'd become and then all the failure started to happen as well. It was one of the toughest moments in my life. Accepting you're not perfect is a real blow to the gut when life sets in. If you haven't reached this place yet, as my mom used to say, just keep living. I now know I will fail more in my

future and that is okay. I am prepared for whatever there is to face in order to get to where I want to be and maintain a love for myself that allows me to be who I am while also loving, respecting, and encouraging others. I wouldn't be here writing this book if it weren't for my experiences. I wouldn't be a motivational speaker if it weren't for my experiences. Anything you can think of that you want to do It IS FOR YOU. Conquer your fears and believe in yourself. It is possible.

CHAPTER SIX
Believe in Yourself

"When you believe in yourself others will follow suit."-L. Hollins

Fall in Love with Yourself

As I went into the Fall Season of 2019 I decided to encourage and promote self-love. I called my challenge the "Fall in Love with Yourself" Challenge. Every single day I posted something positive or encouraging. The goal is to wake up every day, tell yourself something positive, love yourself, encourage yourself, make sure every day you are aware that no matter what you face you are 100% a bad ass.

To be honest with you I had some

really great days and in the words of music sensation Lizzo "I woke up feeling like I just might run for president." Other days weren't the best but I stayed the course. I remember during this same time frame Emanuel and I went on a weeks' vacation to South Padre Island, Texas. It was amazing and I had totally underestimated the island. When we returned home, I had the worst week of bouncing back ever. I had insomnia, and depression started to creep in. I'm telling you this story because I made it through without slipping into depression because of the love I had for myself during that time; the things I woke up telling myself during that time helped me get out of bed and keep moving. I also shared with Emanuel how I was feeling so he was aware that I wasn't sleeping and I wasn't feeling like myself. Here's a funny thing I'll share about this same week and it is the perfect example of how things can either make you laugh or make you feel worse.

Emanuel and I went out to dinner the Wednesday of our first week back at work. This was when I shared with him my mood. At this time, my hormones were all over the place (a symptom of PCOS), I was waking up feeling sad and I wanted to cry over the smallest things. After telling him this, the waiter walked in bringing our naan and olive oil blend. Before touching the bread, I

73

decided I needed to go wash my hands. Once I got in the restroom, I thought I better go ahead and tinkle while I am here. Ladies...guys...readers....I GOT LOCKED IN THE STALL!!! I used the restroom and by the time I was ready to leave, there was no knob on the door and get this...I'd left my freaking phone on the table with Emanuel. I know what you're thinking and the answer is no; NO, I couldn't just crawl under the stall. This was a fancy bathroom where each stall was separated by a floor to ceiling wall and a floor to ceiling door. I was legit stuck. After screaming hello, having a minor panic attack in my head, and nearly freaking out for a second, I pulled myself together and processed. I realized I was wearing my Apple Watch which luckily had phone capabilities. I sent Emanuel a message using my watch and he sent someone in to get me. How embarrassing, right? Wrong, this was freaking hilarious once I was safe and sound back at my table. I told Emanuel they didn't even offer me a free drink after that episode. Ha-ha! So, here I am all these years questioning why I pay Verizon an extra $10 a month for phone capabilities on my watch and now that question has been answered and that $10 a month has finally paid off. Now I know it was for that very moment in my life. I was saved from the stall!

This is a funny story but an important

story. This moment could easily have ruined the day of an already exhausted and depressed person. I could easily have ruined the dinner date with my husband and allowed the sadness to eat up what was left of me. Instead, we were able to look at the situation and laugh about it and though the next day I didn't feel 100% myself but I did feel better. I forced workouts even when I didn't feel like it. I continued stating and sharing my positive affirmations each morning and by the following week I was feeling myself again. Hear me when I tell you depression is a sneaky and nasty mood disorder that is no easy feat to beat. It is something we should catch at the earliest onset possible. When you start feeling a change in your mood, your attitude, or just something is off in general with your body take note and take charge. No, it doesn't always work but we can try. I know very well the impact depression can have on our lives.

Four to Five years ago I was at my lowest when it comes to self-care, self-love, and depression. I was the heaviest I'd ever been and had ignored all of the signs that something wasn't right. I was focused on being a great social worker that I literally lost myself. My body physically started to shut down. By the time I realized something was wrong I was in pain, pre-diabetic, obese, exhausted all of the time, and very unhappy with myself. What I remember most from that time in my life was looking in the mirror each day and hating what I saw. I didn't love myself or the way I looked and I didn't know how that bad energy every morning was negatively affecting me as a person and negatively affecting my health. After being told I was pre-diabetic, I had PCOS with infertility, and I needed to lose weight, I did the work to gain my health back and the love I now have for myself came with it. I knew I didn't want to be this unhappy person forever, I was going to have children, and I wasn't going to be diabetic.

I started the lifestyle change journey, I started talking to my husband more, I started sharing more through blogging, I started yoga and walking which slowly turned into jogging. I changed my entire lifestyle and started choosing me and my health first. I will say writing has changed my life and allows me to get a lot off my chest while helping others at the same time. I also learned that it is okay to say NO. When focusing on my health, working out, and eating right was a must. I had to say no to certain events that cut into my workout time or didn't fit my new lifestyle at the time. I needed to be consistent until I was strong enough to handle it. I also learned to take my own food into restaurants when friends wanted to eat out...maybe it was embarrassing or uncomfortable for them but not for me and I was doing this for me. (Believe it or not I was never approached in any restaurant saying I couldn't bring in my own food). Yes, I lost weight but most importantly I found exactly what I needed to be for myself and my own personal growth. I learned to love the person I was as well as the person I was becoming. I was grateful for ME.

As I write this book today is day 45 of my Fall in Love with Yourself Challenge and what I can say is I don't know if many people are waking up and giving themselves positive affirmations but what I am 100% sure of is every single day they are watching me do it and I think that is inspiring enough. I have had several people reach out and say they are watching and I am affecting their lives in ways I can't imagine and that is enough for me. Self-love and self-care take time. It can feel uncomfortable to people who aren't used to showing themselves the same love they show those they care about. I want to ensure that you know it's okay to wake up and say I. AM. A. BAD. ASS and I. AM. WORTHY! Because damn it you are...WE ALL ARE!

CHAPTER SEVEN
Get Over the Shame and Guilt!

"Shame is much more likely to be the source of destructive, hurtful behavior than the solution or cure."- Brene Brown

You are worthy. You deserve to be loved. You deserve to be happy. You deserve to be an individual. Why did I start this chapter with these four lines? Because, we forget these things about ourselves on a daily basis. There is a clear difference between shame and guilt and one is more detrimental than the other. When discussing shame, we tend to absorb and personalize the hurt or failure. We inflict more pain by feeling like we are the problem and we are

an awful person as opposed to guilt which is,
I made a mistake and I feel bad about that.
One focuses on us as a person and the other
focuses on one individual mistake. An
example would be I stepped on your shoe
and I feel really bad about that versus I
stepped on your shoe and I am an awful
person for that and I don't deserve your
forgiveness. Shame is destructive. Guilt is
constructive.

In discussing self-love, I have to discuss
shame and guilt because it comes within the
territory. When we start putting ourselves
first it's abnormal and we feel bad for
thinking we deserve to do or be anything
else other than what our family needs us to

be. We forget that our family members need us to be happy and present. We can't be anything for them if we are not our best selves. We feel ashamed and we feel guilty for wanting to go someplace without them. We feel bad if we spend a small amount of money on ourselves because we know it could be money used towards something the kids may need in the future. Truth is you deserve a moment to yourself. You deserve a getaway to remember who you are as a person and who you are without all of the roles that weigh so heavily on your shoulders every day. It is neither safe nor is it healthy to function in overdrive every single day of your life. It's okay to want these things and more importantly it is okay to not feel guilty as you enjoy it.

How do you start to shed the shame and guilt as it relates to self-care? You start slow. You include those you love in the process. You educate them on the importance of you having a break and how it allows you to recover. It doesn't have to be this drastic change but it can be taking a day to go to yoga and your husband prepares dinner for the night, handles homework with the kids, and prepares them for baths. It can eventually develop into a quarterly girl's trip or mom getaway. It can look like whatever you need because everyone's daily schedule and life looks different. So, you may need something completely different from me that allows you to feel recovered. Think about what it is that you need and want that will allow you to be the best version of yourself. Put it on paper. Make sure you are clear with what this change will look like so when you share this information with your loved ones they will understand and the plan will be clear; it will also show that you are serious with the amount of time you put into the plan.

CHAPTER EIGHT
Forgiveness of Self

"Mistakes are always forgivable, if one has the courage to admit them."-Bruce Lee

As I mentioned earlier, be kind to yourself and give yourself credit for all that you do and have done. When we make a mistake, we tend to become our very own worst enemy. In order to truly love yourself you have to forgive yourself for all of your past mistakes. Those mistakes you have been beating yourself up about for the last 10 years, forgive yourself and let it ago. The burdens you have consistently carried with you from year to year, dragging you down, making you feel inferior, making you feel unworthy of love, let it go.

The key to letting all of the past hurt and pain go is acceptance of what you did, admitting you were wrong, and making amends. It is also getting comfortable with the idea that the person you hurt may not forgive you but if you do your part you have to forgive yourself. When they are ready to forgive you, they will. You can't walk around hating yourself for a single mistake and you can't continue to punish yourself. Mistakes don't make you a bad person. Mistakes don't mean you can never be happy. Mistakes mean you messed up, you realized it, you apologized, and you moved forward.

It is important to remember apologies

come along with changed behavior. So, when you apologize to someone, you are vowing to do everything in your power to not make the same mistake again. I honestly think this can apply to you as well. If you have been dragging old baggage with you, year after year, relationship after relationship you should apologize to yourself and vow to never do that again. You can't grow and love yourself if you can't forgive yourself for mistakes you've made. Inability to forgive yourself is a form of that destructive shameful behavior we discussed. It continues to weigh you down and make you feel unworthy. You must forgive yourself to move forward.

CHAPTER NINE
Forgiveness of Others

"Forgive others not because they deserve forgiveness, but because you deserve peace." –Jonathan Lockwood Huie.

In the last chapter we discussed forgiveness of ourselves. We know it is the key to being able to move forward in life and truly loving ourselves 100%. Forgiveness of others is another very important part of moving forward in life. I know you are wondering, Lashonda, how do I forgive someone who hurt me to my core. My answer to that is forgiveness is for you not them. I repeat, forgiveness is for you and your ability to grow and move forward. You can never really move forward if you can't forgive those who wronged you.

I can hear you now saying I am completely crazy for even thinking we can forgive some of the horrible acts we've experienced. You don't have to forgive anyone to move on. Deep down you know the truth though. You know every time the name of the person who wronged you is mentioned you cringe. You know you are disgusted at the sound of their name. You know the idea of being in the same room with them is either 1. not going to happen or 2. it is going to make every other person in the room uncomfortable. Why be miserable simply because you can't forgive someone.

The truth is you are holding on to all of the hurt and pain they caused you which is preventing a brighter future for you. True forgiveness doesn't mean we are going to hang out later and be best friends. It simply means you forgive the person for what they did to you so that you can move closer to your destiny. Constantly reliving what someone did to harm you is detrimental to your health. Even if you feel they don't deserve forgiveness you deserve all of the positivity that comes from forgiveness. I use to watch the murder mystery shows and see people say they have forgiven the person who murdered their loved ones and I'd think HOW? It wasn't until later in life that I

realized it's because they have to. In order
not to be bitter or harbor hate they had to.
In order to not remain in a constant state of
grief and sadness they had to find a way to
forgive for their own sanity and their own
peace of mind.

I know a mean-spirited person who
hurt me and some of the people I love but I
have chosen to forgive him. In the past I
harbored so much disregard for the person
that even the site of him made me angry all
over again. I couldn't fathom how a person
could be so nasty and be okay with being
that way. It took me several years to accept
that he is very sick and he also doesn't
forgive. Therefore, he is bitter and carries

hatred, jealousy, and pain around with him all the days of his life and honestly that makes me sad for him. I also know I wasn't 100% innocent in the situation. This is where self-awareness comes in; knowing I could've handled several interactions better than I did. But I chose to not only forgive myself but forgive him as well.

I actually had a dream about this person last month and it wasn't the normal dragging each other across the dinner table dream (ha-ha). I told my husband it was actually a dream and not a nightmare so that says something. The dream alone assured me that I'd truly found peace and forgave the person. After the dream my response was wanting to reach out to him and tell him, "though we will never have the same relationship we had in the past, I still love and I will never stop loving you." Full disclosure, I didn't send the message. I discussed it with a couple of people and made the decision not to open old wounds and accept my peace and move forward.

You will know for sure when you have truly forgiven someone because the thought, mention, or site of them doesn't make your skin crawl or make your blood boil. You either want them to get better and do well or you just be and move on. Just being doesn't even have to include them as a thought; you are truly moving forward with your life. I think until the dream I'd forgiven and moved forward. I was just being. Friends, this is an amazing feeling.

To be in constant defense mode carrying hurt and frustration with you everywhere you go is exhausting. You don't have to experience this. You don't have to do this to yourself. Tell yourself that not letting go of this burden is causing you more pain than happiness and now is the time to truly let go. LET. IT. GO. Truly forgive and feel the weight lifted and the peace that comes along with it.

CHAPTER TEN
Broken Relationships: Life Goes On!

"Letting go of a bad relationship doesn't mean any love was lost. It simply means you've realized the only behavior you can change is yours. Life goes on."-L. Hollins

You can spend an entire life time investing in a relationship that you will never get anything from. So many people both men and women are in relationships that feel safe because they have someone-- anyone. Let me not get ahead of myself. I'll start with a story from our anniversary trip we just got back from. Emanuel and I decided to travel to South Padre Island this past week to celebrate our 9th year of marriage. On our actual anniversary he surprised me with a sunset dinner cruise. Let's face it, we never meet a stranger, so we met a couple on the boat ride and as we sailed, we shared with them what we were celebrating. During the conversation I jokingly said, "I've been with him for 16 years and I still like him." Our new female friend repeated what I said saying, "See she didn't say love. She only said like." As they laughed. Of course, for me, this was a teachable moment and I immediately went into Lashonda Hollins the therapist and out of Lashonda Hollins the vacationer. It's hilarious thinking back to that moment now.

I explained to them that spending 16 plus years with a person you want to make sure you "like" them. You want to make sure you enjoy them. You want to ensure you are their friend. I went on to explain how we can love a person very much but grow apart. You can love a person that you can't stand to be around. You can love a person and not like who they have become. You can love a person whom you feel is an awful person to others. You can love a person who at the thought of being alone with them and trying to have a conversation literally makes you ill. This is why, my friends, it is so important to maintain a friendship with the person you are spending your life with.

So how does this tie into self-love?

Simple. Let me explain. First, I will start with my unwed readers. I have watched so many of you, who are not married, stay in relationships that were broken from day one but you stayed anyway. I have watched you put yourself through so much strife. I have watched you suffer from mental abuse, emotional abuse, psychological abuse, and even physical abuse trying your best to make a toxic relationship work. LISTEN SIS...NO, JUST NO! You are so much better than a dead-end relationship and you deserve so much more than just a warm body that makes you feel like you have someone there with you. The truth is you don't have anyone there with you. Having that person is equivalent to having no one at all if not worse... because of the damage they are causing to your self-worth on a daily basis. You have a person every day you are carrying around with you like a ton of bricks on your back, but in this case, they are tied to your heart. You have a person who doesn't contribute and only takes or they contribute and hold it over your head or controls all the money (financial abuse), lies daily, who treats you like trash, who makes you feel like you are always the problem. Nothing about this relationship says he likes me nor loves me.

I know you are afraid to walk away

from this relationship but stop and ask yourself, what does this person bring to the relationship? What value does this person bring to my life? If you don't have a rock-solid answer then please think about what this relationship is doing to you physically, mentally, and emotionally. I truly believe that people will only do to you what you allow. Once they realize you will take this or that, then they will continue to lay it on thick. Here's an example. If I ask you for money and never pay you back but you keep giving it to me every single time I ask, then you better believe I am going to keep asking you for it. In the words of the great Dr. Maya Angelou, "When a person shows you who they are, believe them." Actions tell you everything you need to know. Trust me, life goes on even if you choose to love yourself more.

Now, for my married readers. In no way am I saying start planning your divorce. What I am saying, though is, if you are in a relationship with a person you love more than anything but you honestly don't like them now is time to do something about it. You have one of two things you can do. The first one is to determine why you don't like your partner anymore and fix it together. This will take a lot of communication, trust, hard truths, and even therapy. People tend to be afraid of hard truths because they have a little bite to them. The self-awareness we talked about in earlier chapters really comes in to play and it's really tested. The work you put in won't be easy and it won't be repaired overnight...in fact it will be HARD and a drawn-out process. It will be downright grueling. There will be days you want to quit and throw in the towel but remember anything worth fighting for is worth having. When you put in the work to repair something so precious you take much better care of it moving forward.

Your second option is, again, determine why you don't have a friendship with the person you love. Do all of the things we mentioned above to try and make things work. If all of the work doesn't end in successful results, there is no way around it, you have to face the fact that it can't be fixed. It's okay if it can't be fixed. You didn't screw it up, you are not a failure, it just didn't work out and you both gave it your best shot. Feeling bad about a failed relationship or marriage doesn't mean you have to stay. It simply means you wanted it so bad to work but reality is it didn't work. That's okay.

What I am trying to get you all to see in this chapter is that life goes on whether you are in the relationship or not. Life is too short to spend it in relationships or friendships that simply don't work. Yes, the same rules can be applied to friendships. Sometimes we find ourselves in friendships where we are constantly giving ourselves and our time to others who don't reciprocate. I have found myself in this place quite often. I am a friend that shows up and supports. I am a friend that expects the same in return and sometimes end up disappointed due to the unrealistic expectations that I have set for people who have only shown me they are unreliable. The fact remains that we can't control their behaviors, they are showing us who they are, we must decide if it is a friendship worth continuing or not. Is there more value than disappointment from the friendship? If you choose to continue you are accepting the behavior and have to be okay with "what you see is what you get" from that friend. The choice is yours.

Another idea I heard recently, which I loved, is if you choose to remain friends with someone who doesn't reciprocate the friendship you give to them, then it is perfectly okay to provide them with what they provide to you. You can't keep giving more and expecting more when you constantly get less. In doing that you set yourself up for constant disappointment and have set unrealistic expectations that will never be met. I'm not saying be a jerk but I am saying if they never make your event then you don't have to jump through hurdles to make theirs. If they stand you up for dinner, then when they plan dinner it doesn't have to be a priority for you; it's okay to say no. It's the only way things will feel as though they make sense. Stop being emotionally available for someone who never takes the time to ask how you are...they are never emotionally available for you. You listen to all of their problems and never have a chance to discuss anything that may be bothering you. It is not fair to you. Choosing to be available as much as another person is available to you is not rude; it's a simple I'm sorry, I gotta run. This prevents constant disappointment in your life. Surround yourself with people who bring joy and fulfillment to your life and always do your best to provide the same to them. Once

you do this you can focus on your happiness.

CHAPTER ELEVEN
Journey to Happiness

"Happiness is a journey. Not a destination."-

Ben Sweetland

What makes you smile? What makes you happy? Now ask yourself how many times have you done that in the last year.

I can openly tell you that traveling makes me happy. I have a job where I naturally have to give my energy to others. I always have to be emotionally available for people who can never be emotionally available for me. I have to hear and see some of the saddest stories one could ever experience in their life. I build rapport and connections with clients and they die. Once I have done all of this at work, I then come home and have to deal with my own daily life issues or struggles. I remember the year my grandmother died. She'd battled with cancer for a while so it was a long journey of not knowing when her time would be up but we could see she was suffering. The week my grandmother died I'd also had to call in a wellness check for a client who was also found dead inside of his home. I experienced two deaths and 2 funerals in the same week. One at work and one in my home life. I don't think there is a social worker out there that will tell you this doesn't affect them. I tell you this because in the field of social work it is so easy to find yourself depleted at the end of the day or at the end of the week and then you still have to come home and be mom, wife, sister, and daughter. You still have to make healthy decisions, workout, and try to call everyone back. It. Is. Exhausting.

When I joined this amazing profession, I was so eager. I knew the textbook quote which was you can't save everyone. But the new social worker in me and the over achieving personality I have that I mentioned in the introduction of this book should let you know I went in with a major "bad ass" mentality. I knew I couldn't save everyone but I damn sure wanted to try. I told myself I could work in any setting with any population. If I had to work through the week and complete documentation on the weekends, then I would. You can imagine this took its toll on me very quickly.

I didn't realize it at the time but I was keeping busy not to deal with the thought of my mother's death which happened 3 years earlier and I'd never properly grieved. We planned her funeral and I rolled right back into school, now work, and life. I found myself telling my husband more and more after work that I'd talked enough for the day and didn't feel like talking. I just wanted to sit in silence and be left alone. This, you guys, was NOT okay. I was NOT okay. Around this time was my first battle with depression. I quickly had to figure out what made me happy and start my journey towards getting there. It just so happens that what lead me towards clarity and happiness was the same for my husband as well. It was the perfect way to ensure I was not neglecting myself but we were not neglecting our marriage as well. We are both travel bugs, which was perfect. When we travel it is our time to gain some clarity, focus on ourselves, and focus on each other. It is a real life reset from life's daily woes and a constant journey to help us with reaching our full potential. Now, we try to take at least 3 trips a year. 2 birthday trips and 1 big anniversary trip. This does not include my girl's trips or his getaways with his friends. We support each other in knowing travel is "our thing" both together and apart.

Your daily job or life schedule may not be like mine but it can be just as stressful. It doesn't matter if you are a stay at home mom or the CEO of a Fortune 500 company, we all have stress and people depending on us. It can all become too much sometimes and you deserve a break from it, you deserve to always focus on what makes you happy.

My happy place can include my husband and it can include me being alone. So, it is important that I make sure you are one hundred percent aware that it is okay for your happy place to only include you. Wanting to be alone and be away from the kids, the husband, coworkers, etc. is normal.

You are not wrong or a bad person for

wanting to get away from it all for a few

days. Your happy place doesn't have to be

extravagant. It can be a hammock in the back

yard. If it is a hammock, then by golly build

the damn hammock.

True happiness comes from within. It

includes dealing with the hard stuff, self-

awareness, forgiveness of self and others,

and trusting the process. There are things

and places that allow the clarity you need to

accomplish all of the aforementioned

objectives. Find what makes your heart

flutter with peace and clarity and there you

will find happiness. When you find it, do it as

often as you desire.

CHAPTER TWELVE
Time to Thrive

"My mission in life is not merely to survive, but to thrive; and to do so with some passion, some compassion, some humor, and some style."-Dr. Maya Angelou

Now that you have determined what makes you happy, are you thriving? Do you even know what makes you thrive? What makes you perform your best even under pressure?

Stagnation has always been a feeling that was just uncomfortable for me. I literally hate stagnation. I've never enjoyed feeling complacent or stuck as if I am not growing in some way. For me thriving looks like activity and personal growth. It looks like me working on new credentials, writing this book or starting a new business. This is what thriving looks like for Lashonda. There are so many things that make my thriving possible.

I can tell you right away, thriving for me also includes yoga. I am my best self when I do yoga on a normal basis. Yoga has truly changed my life. Experiencing all of the women's health issues I did from 2015 to 2016 yoga saved me. I experienced depression and yoga was there to help me stay grounded, I experienced pain from a myomectomy to remove fibroids and yoga got me through every single step of the pain and healing process even if it was just focusing on my breathing. There is a strength in me, people, that I would have never known I had, if it wasn't for yoga. Thanks to an amazing friend who introduced me to yoga and who still inspires me today.

As I write this book not only am I working through a Mindfulness Based Stress Reduction course but I am also considering enrolling in a Mindfulness and Meditation Instructors Course. I think about how easily it could have been to allow the pain and the health issues to break me or break my marriage but instead I rose from the ashes like a phoenix trying to turn all of this pain into passion. I still get discouraged. I still question how I think I can make such a big impact. But I have decided to thrive and defy the odds. I am taking my battle with women's health issues which includes PCOS, infertility, fibroids, depression, and anxiety and turn it into something positive. Something that will inspire women. I chose to write this book on self-love as opposed to women's health issues first because one of the very first things I ever struggled with as a young girl was not feeling pretty enough. I want us to know we are all beautiful and amazing just the way we are. If we can truly believe this, then we can tackle all of the other things' life will throw our way in the next book.

My goal is to inspire women and use

my platform to reach as many women as possible; both young and old alike. This makes me thrive; defying the odds, setting goals and crushing them for women makes me thrive.

CHAPTER THIRTEEN
Set the Foundation

"With a strong foundation you can always build or rebuild on that same foundation."- Jack Scalia.

I have shared a lot of information with you in this book. My goal is to make it something you can implement in your life while sharing a little of my journey along the way. If you are able to actually follow this guide and do the work that comes along with it then you can set the foundation and begin this journey towards complete self-love.

Remember this is a constant and never-ending journey. The road to self-love is a fluid process. It is not fixed and is ever changing. Once you have reached what you believe to be complete self-love the work doesn't stop. There are days I wake up and I still feel fat, I question my abilities, and I sometimes feel like a disappointment to myself and others. Then I remember who I really am. I do the work. I state the facts to myself and that is what I listen to. I refuse to listen to the negative thoughts as they are only meant to break me and tear me down. I know I have accomplished a lot; I know I am not a disappointment, and I know a few extra pounds doesn't define who I am as a person. I focus on all the things I do well. Always remember when you are having a bad day and you are questioning your existence and your abilities, look yourself in the mirror and see the FACTS. You are a beautiful person inside and out. You are capable of doing anything you believe you can do. You deserve every ounce of happiness. You deserve to be here because you earned it. You are loved. You deserve love. This is a continuous journey because depression, sadness, vulnerabilities, and other major life events don't stop. So, as the world continues to move and shift, so do you. Continue to build and rebuild on the same foundation you have built for yourself and if for some reason it should crack, you build another foundation.

CHAPTER FOURTEEN
The Blog Spot

"What you have to say is important. So, say it."-L. Hollins

As this book came to a close, I thought about all of the blog posts I've written over the years and how so many of them would be relatable for my readers who are just being introduced to my work. So here I wanted to give you a piece of my heart and share posts from when I first started writing and developing this passion to empower and encourage others.

R.E.S.P.E.C.T: Find out what it means to me
December 20, 2014

I must begin by apologizing. I have

really been slipping when it comes to my blog posts. I won't make any excuses because though, I have been busy, there have been plenty of opportunities for me to slip in a quick post or 2. I know people enjoy my blogs and I would like to say thank you for being such loyal readers. I will also say I get PLENTY of hits on my "inspirational" posts but not so many on my COCOTIQUE unboxing posts. I thought more people would be interested because it was interesting for me.... lol but I guess everyone isn't as crazy about hair, makeup, polish, and other accessories as I am. With that being said I think I might stop doing unboxing posts. :(But, don't worry the other stuff will keep coming. :)

Question: How important is respect to you? Respect in relationships (Familial, friendship, or romantic relationship)? Receiving respect and giving respect? Watching someone you love disrespect other people? How does it affect your relationships?

I have had something on my heart as it relates to this topic for the last few weeks and today, I started thinking..."What happens when a friend, lover, or family member loses a little of your respect?" There are several ways people can lose some of your respect but for me and my situation, their actions made me see the person in a different light. I still love them and I still consider them to be close to me but at that moment when my respect changed, something in that relationship changed as well. I can't quite put my finger on it but SOMETHING changed.

This was very new for me because I can cut someone off really quick when they have done something to ME! But when they do something that "I wouldn't do to another person," or "something I think is completely wrong" BUT NOT DIRECTLY TO ME that may not "really" be grounds to just cut them off. I always try to make sure that if I can help...I try that first. I also want to make sure I am not being judgmental because I respect the fact that everyone is not like me and won't always do things the way I think they should be done.

I know...I know what you are thinking, "Address it with them...it must be verbalized because they may be unaware that they did anything wrong." This is what I would tell any client I was working with also. I think I have tried to do that in this situation. I also know you can't make a person change and once you have talked and they basically say "oh well...this is what you get" You move on!

I toiled and toiled with this and what I am slowly starting to realize is that you can love someone, you can care for them, and you can be there for them when they need you. If it is something you feel you can live with, then live with it. If it is something you can't live with and it goes against everything you believe and stand for then DON'T live with it and you move on. If that "something" that has changed makes it difficult for you to be around that person then it just may not be something you can live with. Who knows...you could be the person being disrespected? and you definitely don't have to live with that disrespect either. Each day is a learning experience for me. I learn from my experiences and I learn from the experiences of others as well so I am not claiming to have all of the answers...because I don't. I am not claiming that my situation will work out perfectly because I don't know.

131

But one thing I am 100% certain of is: *Life is too short to live it with people you don't really care to be around...people that don't make you happy...people that hurt other people... and people that hurt you!* Live your life happily and live your life to the fullest. Respect is very important within any relationship and when you have lost ALL respect for something or someone it may be time to find the nearest EXIT!!

P.S. Trust that it is okay to love someone from a distance.

Thanks for reading!

Toodles!! XOXO

If You Are Living, Make Sure You Are Learning
January 4, 2015

HAPPY NEW YEAR!!!!!!!!!!!!

It's a new year and this year is not just mine or yours...this year can be each and every one of our year! I pray you have a great intro to 2015 and you plan to do something amazing throughout. I honestly feel that waiting until the new year to begin a "new you" is a cop out...every day you are alive is an opportunity to change your life! :) So, if you missed it on January 1, as of today you still have 361 days left!

This week I saw something very amazing! I was sitting at work and a coworker and friend came into my office and handed me 2 pieces of paper. She said, "hey have you read this? Read it" and handed me the material. So, of course I took it, sat down at my desk and began to read it. It was a blog from someone who had been married for 36 years and it was she and her husband's Anniversary. She titled her post "36 things I know after 36 years of Marriage." For me this was absolutely amazing! It taught me something...I learned!

Each day that you awake, one of your daily goals should be "to learn something." I would love to start jotting down or making mental notes of things I'll learn throughout the year. I would love to ONE DAY create a post sharing what I have learned as it relates to marriage but today, I think I will share what I have learned about life in general. Some people will say at 28 years of age, what have you really learned about LIFE? but I can honestly say I have learned A LOT in my 28 years of living.

28 Things I have learned in 28 years of LIVING!

1. The world owes you nothing.

2. Anything you need you work for and yes, sometimes you may have to work harder than others.

3. Trust yourself and trust that you are worthy.

4. Everything doesn't happen when

you want it but when it does

you will know.

5. Once you stop believing in
   yourself, having someone that
   never stops believing in you by
   your side is important.

6. You only get 1 life...no one has
   the right to tell you how to live
   it.

7. If you are unhappy
   everyday...you need to re-
   evaluate yourself, your life and
   who's in it.

8. Make time for those who make
   time for you.

9. Don't stress about things you

have no control over.

10. Fix the things you can control and pray about the others.

11. Friends don't last forever.

12. The saying "some people are in your life for a season" is VERY true!

13. Never be afraid to ask for help.

14. Asking for help and living off of someone is VERY different. One day your well will run dry.

15. Never forget to take care of yourself...spiritually, emotionally, mentally, and financially.

16. There really are people who

want to see you fail. But there are people that want to see you succeed as well...focus on them.

17. Love YOURSELF...don't depend on another person for your happiness.

18. It takes more energy to be angry and hate someone than it does to forgive them and move on.

19. Forgiveness is FOR YOU not them!

20. Everyone will have opinions...they're just that, OPINIONS!

21. People will always question what and how you're doing things...but they don't have the answer either.

22. Whatever the problem...it will pass.

23. Work Hard...Play hard. :) Treat yourself! Don't work just to live and live just to work.

24. After you become a parent don't let it consume your identity. It's part of you but not ALL of you. You're still a wife/husband, brother/sister, son/daughter, aunt/uncle, friend, lover

of music,   lover

of travel, foodie...etc. You can

still do things you loved to do

and be a parent at the same

time.

25. Shit happens...don't waddle in

it.

26. You are strong and you are

resilient;   remember every

storm has a lesson. There really

is a rainbow after each storm

though some last longer than

others.

27. Never be afraid to grow...don't

let fears hold you back.

28. The hardest lesson I have

learned in all my 28 years is: People don't live forever (duh). The person you think will be here to share moments with can and will leave any day. I never imagined that at 22 years old I would lose my mother. I honestly thought she would be with me forever. We all know that death is inevitable but I never thought it would happen to me so soon. I thought, this happens to other people...not me. Ultimately, I had to grow up. I learned to love harder and cherish the times I do have with the people I love. I take nothing for granted and count it all as a blessing.

Of course, I have learned so much more! I had to choose the important ones and combine some of the others lol. Overall, Life is tough without a doubt...it's sometimes not fair and changes daily. Many may ask, are we ever really prepared to "Take on the World?" I say HECK YEA! Bring it on! I have a purpose...I will live for my purpose!

Throughout this year take the time to admire what you have learned. Take in the good and the bad...absorb it and grow! On day 365 when you ask yourself, "have I learned this year...and have I grown from what I learned? I pray you are able to respond with, "This year I am a better person and a stronger person. I lived and I learned."

Toodles!! XOXO

Self-love: The Most Important
July 25, 2015

Happy Saturday Readers!!!

Today I want to talk about SELF love. If you know me now you would NEVER know I struggled with self-love growing up! Today I am told I am a diva, I am confident, and some may even say boojie. Lol...I promise if you get to know me you will see so much more; judging me by just looking at me is really your loss.

I am going to be verrrry honest with you about the old Lashonda...and I am going to be verrry honest with you later about the new Lashonda.

As a young girl I was tiny, with big boobs (way bigger than anyone else my age), exotropia (when 1 or both eyes turn outward), and darker skin than everyone else. At that age I had no idea how beautiful I was and didn't even know where to start in learning how to love myself. I never let it show but my confidence and my self-esteem were pretty low; I compared myself to EVERYONE ELSE! Mistake #1! I can say I never struggled to have or make friends...popularity was never an issue for me. I had and still have some pretty amazing friends. All my issues revolved around "self."

In 11th grade I met my now husband; the first person that ever said to me "you're beautiful just the way you are." For me this was major and it still took time for me to believe him. What I now understand after my years of education is that someone can tell you you're beautiful, smart, and talented every day of your life but it is not until YOU believe it that the changes start to happen. Don't get me wrong, them telling you this is a start and makes you feel all bubbly inside...but the real work comes when you start to believe it and say it yourself. Self-love is sooo important women; it impacts our lives in soo many ways! You would be very surprised how many people wear the "I'm happy and beautiful" exterior but on the inside, they are broken and hate who they are.

I always wanted to change things about myself but I knew I loved myself (without my husband's input) the day I was told I could have surgery to straighten my eye and I said NO. This, you guys, was one of the things I hated about myself THE MOST; but on that day I chose to love myself just the way God made me. Over time I have had to DO THE WORK, as Iyanla would say. (LOL) I chose to trust that I was beautiful.

For a while as a young adult I thought I was too "dark" to wear red and pink lipsticks...now I am bolder...now I trust I'm perfect with whatever I choose to wear.... I make my clothes and my lipsticks...I don't let them make me. I now know that MY BLACK IS BEAUTIFUL! I chose to love myself FIRST and not think about what the world would say first! Of course, this new weight gain has been a hard pill to swallow but again I went back to doing the work and that's where I am today.

Today I really am a different person. Not only did I change internally but when that happened things changed externally as well. I carry myself differently. What others say about me doesn't really matter. I don't live to please others and I live for LASHONDA! The new Lashonda takes risks without being afraid. What about you?

**Stay Pretty and Love yourself **

Toodles!

The Importance of Forgiveness
December 28, 2016

Hey y'all!!

I wasn't feeling too hot today so instead of just sitting around I thought why not write a blog to close out the year.

Something has been on my heart for the last week or 2 and today I saw a status on Facebook about something very similar so I took that as a sign. So, I'd like to talk about forgiveness and why it's important to forgive those who have wronged you.

I'll be the first to admit that forgiveness hasn't always been my strong area. I could easily move on, shut people out, shade them when I see them, and keep it moving. But recently forgiveness hit me like a ton of rocks. I felt happier, lighter, and overall, I just felt good...a weight really had been lifted. I've always said forgiveness isn't for the other person it's for YOU. But in saying that I always remained a little hypocritical because I wasn't truly forgiving ALL of those individuals that I felt have wronged me. Today I can honestly say I have forgiven.

I refuse to go into 2017 with anger and bitterness in my heart. I've seen firsthand what holding anger, bitterness, and grudges in one's heart looks like. You end up being an ugly person and it shows on the outside as well as destroys you on the inside. It can even destroy other relationships around you. I refuse to become that person. SO, I FORGIVE YOU...and I pray if I've wronged anyone, they can forgive me as well. Not for me but for themselves.

So, take a look around you and see how much energy you waste on being bitter with a mother or father that was never there, a friend that let you down, a sibling, a child's father.... anyone!! Now imagine how you'd feel if you let it all go. If you didn't get angry every time you were around them, every time you see their name, or someone talked about them in your presence. It truly feels amazing. You can walk out of a room knowing you did your part and you feel good about it. That's what matters and that's the feeling you want.

So, I challenge you to go into 2017 with all weight and bitterness lifted. Forgive those people and pray that they forgive you. Move forward with your life and take nothing for granted.

Choose Love...every single time. ♥ Forgiveness shows your strength.

Ephesians 4:31- "Get rid of all

bitterness, rage and anger, brawl and slander, along with every form of malice."

XOXO

Lashonda

Check On the strong ones
March 19, 2018

Last week I came across a meme that stated something along the lines of "check on your strong friends." It's crazy because I immediately thought about myself. I don't naturally share what's going on in my life with people. Often times I think I am handling it (along with everyone else's problems) ... until I am not. One major lesson I learned over the last year is not to get

152

involved in other people's drama. At the end of the day I am the one stressed and the next week they're out here LIVING and doing the same things they were just complaining to me about! lol but I am getting off subject. So back to checking on your strong friends...

Over the last year my home life has been absolutely amazing. I have the best husband in the world. But let's face it my work life has been causing me sooo much stress and only a handful of people were aware of this. Only a handful of people were aware that I started having anxiety attacks at work and started medication to deal with it (hence my inability to lose these 15 pounds). For a while I couldn't understand why everything was going so right at home but so wrong at work. The attacks were only happening at work. During the time that my anxiety attacks started we'd lost over half of our staff at work. I'd been trying to switch departments/positions for a while and nothing seemed to work. I am not a person that likes complacency. I felt stagnate. One day I was SO busy covering 2 caseloads, my work phone wouldn't quit ringing and everything with everyone seemed to be going wrong. I nearly ran a stop sign with a client in the car with me. This was when the attacks started. This was when I realized life was moving too fast. That evening I went home feeling completely beat down and overwhelmed. I thought "let me just look at this phone and see how many times it rang." My work phone had rung 50 times in ONE day!!

I talked to Emanuel and we agreed I should see a doctor, I started yoga back religiously, and did some self-assessing. I quickly realized it wasn't the work that was causing my anxiety, I'd done this job for nearly 5 years. It was a combination of not wanting to do it anymore, burnout, disappointment, and my NEED to still be PERFECT. My need to still solve all the problems, answer every phone call, and save every life even though double the lives were calling. I'd been told several times before that I am a perfectionist and for me that had always been a good thing...until it wasn't.

After several vacations, some self-care, and another big slap in the face I realized I needed to take my life back because this job wasn't going to kill me. If I have to take pills everyday just to go to work...then work isn't worth it anymore.

I am happy to say that I am no longer on anxiety medication, haven't had an anxiety attack in months, and will be starting a new job in less than 1 month. I will be moving to San Antonio to do it but that's okay by me. God is placing Emanuel and I right where we need to be. We are having to make sacrifices again as we do every time things start to shift in our lives and God is setting us up for something greater. Wherever He leads I will follow.

I say all of this to say check on your STRONG friends sometimes...sometimes we have it all together but sometimes we don't. Sometimes we may say we are fine...even when we are not.

XOXO

Lashonda Hollins

Borrowed Time
December 31, 2017

Happy New Year's Eve!!!! 2017 is coming to an end and Snapchat reminded me of just how much I have done this year and I felt fulfilled. Soon after I had that feeling my sister called me with some heartbreaking news about someone I love dearly and we are not sure they will enter into the New Year with us. It's like no matter how much you smile life reminds you we are all on borrowed time.

Borrowed time is my reason for living my best life. Emanuel and I have a hard time with choosing to be there for someone else verses choosing to be there for ourselves (he is a little worse at this than me). This year we decided not to feel bad about choosing ourselves and it was honestly the best thing we could have ever done. It is so easy to get caught up in doing for others, being there for others, LIVING for others, and forget about living for yourself. Don't get me wrong there is nothing wrong with being supportive of others but that shouldn't be your single purpose in life. Over time E and I have realized that we are ALWAYS there for others and ALWAYS traveling to see them but out of all of the states we have lived in, even when we were in Mississippi, I can count on 1 hand how many family members or friends have made an effort to come and visit us. Don't get me wrong I understand there are circumstances that prevent people from being as present as we would like them to be in our lives but I also know there can be absolutely none as well.

I am sharing this because someone out there is further off than me and 2018 needs to be YOUR YEAR to use your time wisely. You are choosing to be something you're not, choosing to be in a relationship that was dead years ago, choosing to stay when you know you should go, choosing someone else's feelings and happiness over yours and you have been doing it for too long.

I don't usually ask much of my readers but today I really want you to ask yourself these questions aloud. Ask yourself, "Am I happy?" Ask yourself, "Am I living my best life? Have I done at least 1 thing this year I have always dreamed of doing?" Lastly, ask yourself "If my borrowed time ran out today could I say, "I have lived my best life, I have lived a fulfilled life and I HAVE NO REGRETS?" If you answered "no" to any of those questions, this year is your year to make those changes. 2018 is the year that you can use your borrowed time and choose to do something for yourself.

We are all on borrowed time. How you plan to use it is up to you.

XOXO

Lashonda

CHAPTER FIFTEEN
Write Your Own Story

This is where the work begins for you.

I am providing you with the space you need

to set your foundation and write your own

story. You will begin with what you would

like total self-love to look like. It's like setting

a goal for yourself and then building the

action plan towards getting there. Use these

next pages to start being exactly who you

want to be and who you were meant to be.

I'm routing for you.

Best of Luck,

Lashonda

XOXO

Your Journey begins here

What Self-Love Looks Like for Me....

_____

_____

_____

_____

_____

_____

_____

_____

_____

_____

_____

_____

_____

_____

_____

_____

_____

What are the Facts?
I deserve to be here because...

_____

_____

_____

_____

_____

_____

_____

_____

_____

_____

_____

_____

_____

_____

_____

I deserve to be loved because...

_____

_____

_____

_____

_____

_____

_____

_____

_____

_____

_____

_____

_____

_____

_____

_____

_____

I am a good person because...

_____

_____

_____

_____

_____

_____

_____

_____

_____

_____

_____

_____

_____

_____

_____

I need to

forgive_____for_____and

because...

_____

_____

_____

50 Positive Affirmations...

Repeat one or two of these daily. Set your intentions and speak positivity into your life.

1. I AM a bad ass!

2. I AM worthy.

3. I may be bruised but I AM NOT broken.

4. I AM capable of doing anything.

5. I AM capable of BEING anything I want to be.

6. Today will be a great day.

7. Today I will bring joy to someone's life.

8. Today I will have peace and serenity.

9. Today I will overflow with greatness.

10. Today I will achieve greatness.

11. I am a work in progress and that is okay.

12. I am a success story.

13. I am growing, achieving, and thriving.

14. I am the world's greatest.

15. I am doing my best and my best is good enough.

16. I AM good enough.

17. I deserve to be treated with dignity and respect.

18. I deserve this job and this raise.

19. I am a rock star and a powerhouse.

20. I can conquer any fear.

21. No obstacle is too big for me.

22. I am always respectful.

23. I always carry myself with dignity and respect.

24. I am always courteous, kind, and

graceful.

25. I have so much to be grateful for in my life.

26. I have so much to look forward to.

27. I am a beautiful person inside and out.

28. Whatever this day entails I will come out on top.

29. I am a winner.

30. Change your thoughts change your day.

31. I see the best in me.

32. I love you.

33. I am valuable.

34. I am safe.

35. I am intelligent.

36. Life is beautiful.

37. I will slay this day.

38. Winners don't quit.

39. Keep Pushing!

40. Never give up on yourself.

41. I am important too.

42. I have the power to make the change.

43. Confidence is beautiful.

44. Never be intimidated.

45. You deserve the desires of your heart.

46. Happiness starts within.

47. Other people's opinions of me don't matter.

48. I am proud of the person I am and the person I am becoming.

49. It's okay to say no.

50. I am allowed to change my mind.

Made in the USA
Coppell, TX
28 May 2020

26615389R00115